PA                                                        ds

# PAULA PRYKE'S
# wreaths &
# garlands

**Paula Pryke**
**photography by James Merrell**

RYLAND
PETERS
& SMALL

LONDON NEW YORK

First published in the United States in 1998
and reissued with amendments in 2004
by Ryland Peters & Small, Inc.
519 Broadway, 5th Floor
New York NY 10012
www.rylandpeters.com

Printed in China

Library of Congress Cataloging-in-Publication Data
Pryke, Paula.
  [Wreaths & garlands]
  Paula Pryke's wreaths & garlands / Paula Pryke ;
photography by James Merrell.
      p. cm.
  ISBN 1-84172-723-7
  1. Wreaths.  I. Title: Paula Pryke's wreaths and
garlands. II. Title: Wreaths & garlands. III. Title.
  SB449.5.W74P78 2004
  745.92'3--dc22
                    2004001848

*For this edition:*
**Designer** Megan Smith
**Editors** Clare Double and Lesley Malkin
**Production** Paul Harding
**Art Director** Gabriella Le Grazie
**Publishing Director** Alison Starling

**Illustrator** Helen Smythe
**Stylists** Martin Bourne, Margaret Caselton,
Nato Welton

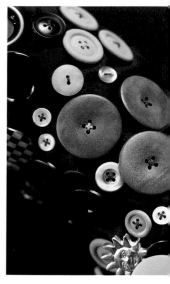

# contents

# introduction

Throughout the world, in every culture, circles, rings, wreaths, garlands, and swags of fresh and dried plant materials have always been steeped in symbolism and meaning. The wreath, in particular, has come to signify eternal love, friendship, remembrance, and even life itself. At both religious and secular events, these decorations have had a role to play—floral headdresses were worn by both bride and groom as a symbol of purity, and flower garlands were, and still are, offered as a greeting to guests in many countries.

Although the craft of wreath- and garland-making dates back to ancient Greece and Rome, it is still popular today, having never really disappeared from our collective experience. By weaving flowers into wreaths, we are continuing a long tradition of designing circular forms for healing or spiritual well-being as well as for their own esthetic value.

Contemporary wreaths, garlands, and swags are essentially flower arrangements without containers and are designed to be displayed on or around doors or walls, draped around parasols and table edges, or worn as headdresses by brides and bridesmaids. Whatever its intended location or use, the modern wreath most commonly maintains its traditional circular shape, but can also be in the form of a heart or novelty shape, and is often associated with remembrance and respect for the dead. Garlands of flowers and foliage,

on the other hand, have happier associations. These long, flexible floral decorations are suspended horizontally or vertically from architectural or garden features. Large-scale garlands of fresh flowers are curled around pillars, tent poles, or staircase banisters for dramatic effect, or hung in dainty chains around a table edge. Swags are typically vertical hanging decorations, but they tend to be shorter and more compact than garlands. Often swags are simply hand-tied bunches of flowers that rely on the plant stems for support rather than being attached to a rigid or flexible wreath base.

The true craft of wreath-making is taking whatever is plentiful and inexpensive in nature and fashioning it into an imaginative decoration. Take pleasure in collecting objects, such as pebbles and driftwood from the seashore, and enjoy the fact that each new season brings fresh materials for wreath-making. Even before I worked professionally with flowers, I took great delight in making fresh and dried displays from mushrooms and moss and other plant matter that I gathered on woodland walks. I particularly relished the season of fall, when I could create simple wreaths out of autumn leaves. Even though these displays were not extravagant or beautifully constructed, there was a sense of achievement in making my own decorations for the home.

Although the following pages are full of inspirational ideas and projects, I hope you will look upon them as a starting point for your own designs. I came to floristry after a career in teaching history and never considered myself artistic. Now that I work with flowers every day, I am constantly amazed at how each individual brings his or her own feel and look to a display even when starting out with identical materials. I think the secret of success is having the confidence to express your style. It is also important to plan the display to suit its location. Whether fresh or dried, wreaths and garlands are among the most beautiful natural embellishments we can bring into our lives. They are timeless art forms that we can make for ourselves and our friends.

# room decorations

Festoons of flowers, foliage, herbs, and fruit were first brought into the home to celebrate harvest and to dry and store seeds; they are one of the earliest forms of floral display. Later, swags of decorative fruit and flowers became popular architectural details in room interiors and were carved from stone or wood or molded from plaster. Today, the use of fresh wreaths as room decorations has undergone a revival— they are used to stunning effect as door, wall, and table ornaments.

ABOVE Freeze-dried roses and bunches of dried lavender and marjoram make for a long-lasting, scented display. The heart-shaped base is wired to a pole and inserted into a dry floral foam-filled pot. LEFT A cornucopia-shaped basket is decorated with sun-dried seedheads and strands of snake grass. Crown imperials fill a plastic container of water set into the basket to make a special door decoration.

**ABOVE AND RIGHT** These attractive paper flowers and dried and dyed red maize were bought from Native Americans in Arizona. I have attached these treasures to a twig wreath sprayed blue as a reminder of the use of color in the Southwest.

**OPPOSITE TOP LEFT** Crab-apples last well in displays. Here, they have been wired to a dry floral foam ring, to offer a warm welcome at a fall gathering.

**OPPOSITE TOP CENTER** Adapt an old wreath frame to create a living wreath of fresh green baby's tears plants. To do this, remove the foam, drill drainage holes in the base, and fill with soil and plants.

**OPPOSITE TOP RIGHT** Hydrangea flowerheads turn burgundy in the fall. Packed into a floral foam ring, they dry naturally to form a permanent display.

**LEFT** Twig wreath bases provide the foundation for many fresh floral displays. Here, small vials of water are wired to the base to keep bachelor's buttons and scabious alive. Trailing ivy hides the base, and shells add interest.

**BELOW** For a modern Shaker-style decoration, simply cut Styrofoam™ into three star shapes and glue red mung beans onto each one. Hang the stars from red ribbon on wooden coat pegs.

# seashell and starfish wreath

This permanent wreath design introduces a nautical theme to bathroom decoration. Select a mixture of mother-of-pearl, scallop, oyster, clam, and spiral shells in a variety of shapes and sizes, and juxtapose their intricate patterns and smooth finishes with spiky, textural starfish and coils of heavy-duty rope.

**MATERIALS & EQUIPMENT**

2 circular wire frames, 30-inch (75-cm) diameter

10 yards (9 m) rope, 2-inch (5-cm) diameter

4 pieces driftwood, 16 inches (40 cm) long

6 mother-of-pearl shells • 2 yellow clam shells

3 cream conch shells • 7 brown-and-white striped conch shells

9 pearl-white spiral cones • 7 long brown spiral cones

4 oyster shells • 1 brown-and-white spiky shell

5 large brown mussel-type shells • 5 large cream mussel-type shells

11 large starfish • 11 small starfish • 8 fan-shaped scallop shells • selection of small shells

spool wire • wire cutters • scrap paper • silver spray paint • hot glue gun and glue sticks

1 Place one circular wire frame on top of the other. Bind the two frames together with spool wire to make an extra-strong base to take the weight of the rope and shells. Lay the double frame on scrap paper, spray it with silver paint, and leave it to dry.

2 Hold one end of the rope and start coiling it loosely over the wire frame in an anticlockwise direction; make sure that the rope encircles the frame at least four times.

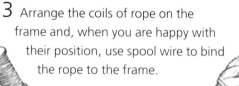

3 Arrange the coils of rope on the frame and, when you are happy with their position, use spool wire to bind the rope to the frame.

4 Evenly space the four pieces of driftwood around the wreath and then glue them securely into place on the rope.

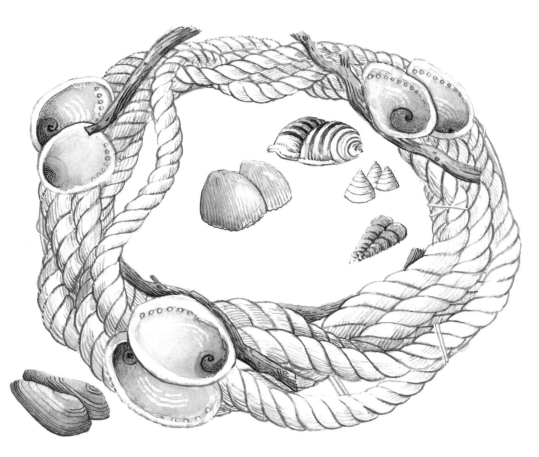

5 Decide which point is the top of the display, and then start by gluing the larger shells onto the rope. Arrange the shells either in pairs or groups of three, and try to balance the colors and shapes around the circular display.

6 Decide where the starfish will have maximum impact and glue them into position. Save the scallop shells until last, and then use them to fill in spaces between the wire frame and rope.

7 Hide any sections of the wire frame that are still visible by gluing small shells onto the frame in groups. When the glue is dry, hang the finished wreath on the wall from a sturdy nail.

1 Take the center of the length of purple rope and, using spool wire, bind the rope to the top of the wreath in two places so the finished display will hang straight.

2 Place one end of the hessian ribbon on the base of the heart and, working in a clockwise direction, arrange the ribbon in decorative folds over the wreath base. Apply dabs of glue to the underside of the hessian ribbon to hold the folds in position.

3 Wire small bunches of lavender on double-leg mounts. Hold a floral wire behind the stems and bend it into a hairpin, making one leg longer than the other. Wrap the long leg of wire around the stems and the short leg at least three times, then bring the wires together.

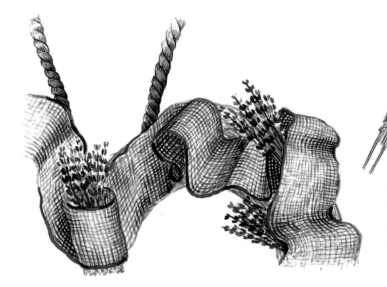

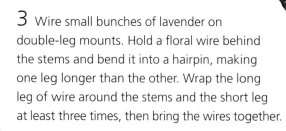

4 Tuck the wired lavender bunches between the ribbon folds and push the floral wires through the wreath base. Bend the wires back on themselves and glue the stems to the heart to anchor the bunches in place.

5 Using floral scissors, snip off the stems of the roses close to the base of the flower. Next, glue the rose heads onto the heart base, attaching some singly and grouping others in clusters.

6 Finish by arranging the galax leaves in groups around the dried roses and lavender. Tuck the galax leaf stems under either the flowers or ribbon and glue them into position.

# horseshoe of succulents

A symbol of good luck in many cultures, the horseshoe is an attractive shape for this wreath created with a variety of succulent species. These popular house and garden plants are ideal subjects for "living wreaths" since, once their roots are embedded in a damp mossy base, they need only small quantities of water and nutrients to survive.

**MATERIALS & EQUIPMENT**

¼-inch (5-mm) chicken wire, 1 x 4 feet (120 x 30 cm)

damp sphagnum moss

plastic bag

30 mixed succulent plants (*Echeveria*)

floral scissors • spool wire • wire cutters

U-pins • medium-gauge floral wires

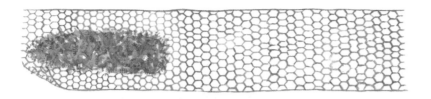

1 Lay the strip of chicken wire flat on the work surface and place a clump of damp sphagnum moss at one end.

2 Tease the moss along the center of the chicken wire and, as you work, wrap the edges around the moss. Then, using spool wire, tightly bind the chicken wire to create a sausage shape. Add further clumps of moss, working your way along the length of the chicken wire, adding extra moss when you reach the center to make it fatter there.

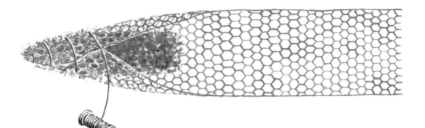

3 When you have completed the sausage shape, knot and cut the spool wire. Next, trim back any straggly pieces of moss so the moss sits close to the frame.

4 Bend the two ends of the sausage shape together to make a horseshoe. Then, turn the frame over and line the back with plastic to prevent the damp moss from damaging the wall. To do this, cut up a plastic bag into several 4-inch (10-cm) strips. Fasten a strip of plastic to the top edge of the horseshoe with a U-pin. Fold the plastic in a zigzag, pinning as you go, so that it follows the edge of the frame. Work your way around the back of the horseshoe until it is covered in plastic.

5 Gently lift each succulent plant out of its pot to keep the roots intact. Shake off any soil. Wire each plant on a double-leg mount by holding a medium-gauge floral wire behind the stem and bending it into a hairpin shape with one leg longer than the other. Wrap the long leg of wire around the stem and short leg, then bring the two wires together. Make sure the wires are long enough to push through the wreath.

6 Begin by attaching the larger succulents to the horseshoe. To attach the plants, hold the floral wires at a 45° angle to the base and push them through the moss. Bend the wires back on themselves to anchor the plant.

7 Keep wiring the larger succulent plants to the horseshoe as described in step 6. Space the plants evenly around the frame to balance the display.

8 Continue wiring plants to the frame, using the technique shown in step 6. Try to balance the colors, sizes, and textures of the different succulents. Last, fill in any gaps on the horseshoe with smaller plants. Spray-mist the display with water every two weeks to keep the moss base moist. This way, the rooted succulents will have a longer life.

# gardening-theme wreath

For the gardening enthusiast, a wreath decorated with seed packs, scarecrow dolls, gnomes, flowerpots, watering cans, and other novelty items makes an original and personal gift. Hung on the shed or kitchen door, it will be a constant source of delight throughout the gardening year.

**MATERIALS & EQUIPMENT**

circular twig wreath, 20-inch (50-cm) diameter

1 stem honeysuckle vine (*Lonicera*), approximately 10 feet (3 m) long

dried carpet moss

5 novelty watering cans

5 small terracotta flowerpots

2 miniature fences

4 pieces driftwood, 6–8 inches (15–20 cm) long

garden trowel and fork

3 yards (3 m) beige burlap ribbon, 2 inches (5 cm) wide

10 dried mushrooms • 5 packs of seeds

3 garden gnomes, 3½ inches (9 cm) tall • 4 scarecrow dolls, 3½ inches (9 cm) tall

spool wire • medium-gauge floral wires • wire cutters • glue

1 Tie one end of the honeysuckle vine to the back of the frame with spool wire and then wrap the length of vine around the twig frame. Next, secure the end of the vine to the back of the circular frame with spool wire.

2 Turn the wreath face up and arrange seven or eight clumps of dried carpet moss on the circular frame. Tuck the moss beneath the threads of vine to hold them in place. For extra security, tie on the moss with spool wire.

3 Arrange the watering cans around the wreath and attach them to the frame with medium-gauge floral wires. To do this, bend a wire around a watering-can handle and push both legs of wire through the twig frame. Twist the ends of wire together at the back and tuck them into the twigs.

4 Next, wire up the pots as follows: bend a medium-gauge floral wire into a loop and twist the ends together. Thread the wires through the drainage hole and pull them through so the wire loop sits in the flowerpot base.

5 Place the wired-up pots on the wreath as two pairs and one single. Attach the pots by threading the wires through the frame and turning them back on themselves. Glue moss into the base of each pot.

6 Wire the miniature fences in the same way as the watering cans. Attach them to the frame at the 4 o'clock and 8 o'clock positions, using the technique described in step 3. Next, glue pieces of driftwood to the frame. Place them at the top, bottom, left, and right. Continue by using spool wire to bind on the tools. Place the tools at the bottom of the wreath, right of center.

7 Glue a piece of moss over the wire that attaches the fork and trowel to the wreath. Next, weave burlap ribbon loosely around the decorative items. Glue the underside of the ribbon folds to the wreath base.

8 Continue by gluing pairs of dried mushrooms to the frame. Next, glue on the seed packs, tucking their corners behind the other decorations. Finally, glue a gnome to the inside edge of each flowerpot and secure the scarecrows by skewering their spikes through the twig base.

# driftwood frame

Wood gnarled and bleached by the sun adds a primitive beauty to any room interior, and here, a rectangular wire frame offers a rigid base on which to show off these driftwood treasures. The beauty of this arrangement is that it is simple and inexpensive to produce and works well as a unique and eye-catching detail. Half the fun of this creation is collecting the material from a park or seashore and piecing together this woody jigsaw puzzle.

**MATERIALS & EQUIPMENT**

rectangular wire frame, 24 x 18 inches (60 x 45 cm)

8 large pieces of driftwood

40 driftwood twigs

1 large, flat pebble

fine-grit sandpaper

spool wire • wire cutters

natural string • scissors

hot glue gun and glue sticks

1 Lay out your pieces of driftwood and the rectangular wire frame on a flat, non-scratch surface. Work out the best way to arrange the wood on the frame; the largest piece will probably look best along the bottom edge. Using fine-grit sandpaper, smooth away any protrusions on the underside of the wood pieces so they will lie flush with the frame.

2 Using spool wire, bind each piece of wood securely onto the wire frame and then cut the wire. Fasten the longer pieces of wood at both ends to hold them in position on the frame.

3 To disguise the sections where wood has been tied onto the frame with spool wire, wind natural string around the wire and fasten it in place with a double knot before cutting it with scissors.

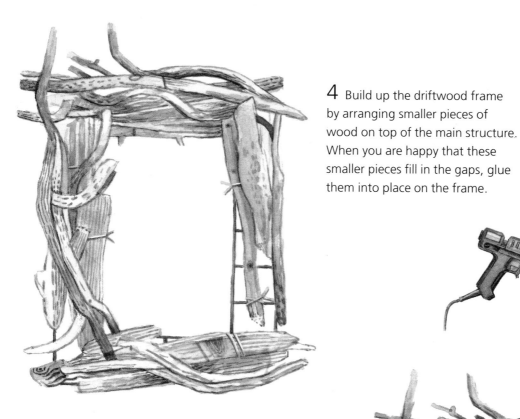

4 Build up the driftwood frame by arranging smaller pieces of wood on top of the main structure. When you are happy that these smaller pieces fill in the gaps, glue them into place on the frame.

5 Finish the frame by gluing on small twigs. Use the twigs to fill any gaps between the larger pieces of wood and also to hide areas where the wire frame is still visible.

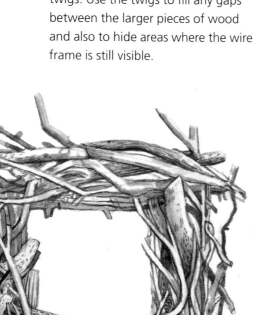

6 Finally, glue the large pebble onto the bottom left-hand corner of the frame. When the glue is dry, hang the frame on a nail, or tie a loop of spool wire to the frame and hang it from a strong picture hook.

# silk-covered button ring

Put your sewing skills to the test by creating this striking purple silk ring studded with an assortment of buttons. Inspired by the fruit and vegetable sellers of London, England, known as the pearly kings and queens, who were famous for decorating their clothes with a lavish collection of pearl buttons, this wreath is both rich and textural.

## MATERIALS & EQUIPMENT

circular twig wreath, 22-inch (55-cm) diameter

2 strips heavyweight (8-ounce/225-g) batting, 14 x 70 inches (35 x 175 cm), joined end-to-end

purple raw silk, sufficient for a strip 15 x 70 inches (37.5 x 175 cm)

200 buttons in a selection of colors, shapes, and sizes

1 yard (1 m) red rope, ½-inch (1-cm) diameter

scissors • needle • straight pins

purple thread plus an assortment of other colors

1 Wrap the strip of batting tightly around the twig wreath like a bandage, to form a padded base. Make sure the edges of the fabric overlap one another so none of the wreath is visible.

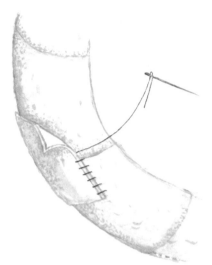

2 When the wreath is covered, trim the end of the batting and baste it in place with a row of neat stitches.

3 Hem the two ends of the strip of silk together. Then lay the silk in a circle on your work surface right side down. Place the "bandaged" wreath on top. Adjust the silk so the ring sits in the center, arranging the inner edge in even folds until you are happy with the way the silk fits.

4 Bring a section of the purple silk around the padded ring. Fold both raw edges of the silk under, tuck the outer edge underneath the inner edge, and then pin them in place.

**5** As you work your way around the wreath, to accommodate the circular shape, you will need to pleat the fabric together, creating neat tucks in the silk at regular intervals. Continue bringing the edges of the silk together and pinning them in place until the ring is completely covered.

**6** Using purple thread, carefully sew the seam together using slipstitch. Take care to remove the pins as you sew.

**7** To form a strong loop, coil the length of rope three times around your hand. Tie the ends of the triple loop together and sew it onto the back of the wreath in the center.

**8** Turn the wreath face up and, using a selection of different colored threads, sew all the buttons to the front of the wreath. Arrange the buttons in groups according to their color, shape, and size.

ABOVE This traditional kissing ball is made by wiring sprigs of mistletoe into damp sphagnum moss in two hanging baskets. LEFT Corn is an important symbol in Thanksgiving celebrations; here, groups of dried cobs are tied with brightly colored raffia to a circular twig frame.

# seasonal wreaths

For thousands of years, the variety and abundance of flowers, fruits, and foliage available at different times of the year have been used to mark the great seasonal events. During the winter months, pine and mistletoe are plentiful and consequently form the backbone of Christmas displays, while golden corn and wreaths of leaves celebrate the fall. In spring and summer, the wealth of fresh flowers available allows us to produce floral displays which are stunning.

OPPOSITE TOP Shimmering silver and purple ribbon, as well as orange fruits and spices decorate this blue fir wreath.
TOP OF PAGE Preserved magnolia leaves maintain their glossy dark green sheen and distinctive shape and look stunning on their own in a classic-style wreath.

CENTER LEFT A snowflake frame of blue fir is simple to make; just wire six plant stakes together with spool wire at the center point, and add the foliage.
BOTTOM LEFT To make a "living wreath," bind potted plants to a frame. Miniature roses here take pride of place on a wall.

ABOVE These mixed colored ranunculi, with their dark centers, are one of my favorite flowers because of their cheerful faces. Bind the stems with rope and pack them in a jar of water covered by sacking. Tie them to the gate to indicate to guests where the party is being held.

# candle centerpiece

Candlelight adds to the special atmosphere when you entertain outdoors. Here, a mosaic-style hurricane lamp is encircled by a rich mix of indigo delphiniums, and purple bluebells and anemones, offset by white ranunculi and starflowers, and green guelder rose and ivy to make a striking centerpiece. By covering the candle with a hurricane lamp, you can keep the flame alive in a breeze and prevent molten wax from dripping over the flowers and table.

### MATERIALS & EQUIPMENT

glass mosaic hurricane lamp and votive candle

circular floral foam base, 15-inch (37.5-cm) diameter

6 stems fruiting ivy (*Hedera*), 2 groups of 3

9 sprigs guelder rose (*Viburnum opulus*), 3 groups of 3

14 purple anemones (*Anemone coronaria*), 2 groups of 7

8 white ranunculi (*Ranunculus*)

10 starflowers (*Ornithogalum montanum*), 2 groups of 5

10 blue delphiniums (*Delphinium* 'Blue Bees'), 2 groups of 5

10 bluebells (*Scilla*)

floral knife • floral scissors

1  Soak the foam base in water for five minutes. Then, using a floral knife, shave off about 1 inch (2.5 cm) from both the inner and outer top edge of the foam in order to give the ring a beveled profile.

2  Cut six stems of fruiting ivy, 3½ inches (8 cm) long. Make two small sprays of three stems each, and then insert the two groups into the foam base at the 12 o'clock and 9 o'clock positions.

3  Make three sprays of guelder rose by cutting the stems to 3½ inches (8 cm) and removing the leaves. Insert two groups of guelder rose next to the two groups of ivy, and the third spray in the 4 o'clock position on the base.

4  Next, add the larger flowers. Cut the stems of the anemones and ranunculi to 2 inches (5 cm). Divide the anemones into two groups of seven flowers and, working from the outer to the inner edge of the ring, place them at 2 o'clock and 6 o'clock. Insert the ranunculi as one group at the 10 o'clock position.

5 Continue with the delicate starflowers, delphiniums, and bluebells. Cut all the stems to 3½ inches (8 cm) long, removing the leaves. Divide the starflowers and delphiniums into two groups. Place each group of starflowers next to the groups of anemones on the ring. Add the delphiniums at the 5 o'clock and 11 o'clock positions. Insert a single group of bluebells into the 7 o'clock position on the circular floral foam base.

6 Make sure the entire base is filled in with fresh flowers and foliage, and then place the display in situ. Carefully put the candle-holder base and votive candle in the center of the flower ring. Light the candle with a taper and cover with the hurricane lamp.

1 Figure out how much string you need by taking it round the bottom edge of the parasol. Leave enough slack in the string to create a generous swag of flowers and foliage between each spoke. Allow a further 12 inches (30 cm) at each end of the string to tie the garland to the parasol.

2 Soak the cut stems in clean water for up to 12 hours. Cut the stems of the flowers and foliage to 8-inch (20-cm) lengths. Strip off the lower leaves and, on a work surface, organize the plant matter into groups, according to type.

3 Start binding flowers and foliage onto the string, 12 inches (30 cm) from one end. Lay a sunflower stem against the string and bind it on tightly with spool wire. Next, place a bunch of fruiting ivy on top of the sunflower stem, close to the flowerhead, and bind this on with spool wire. Follow the ivy with two or three stems of chilies. As you work, cut off the stem ends to make it easier to attach the next group.

4 Continue by wiring on sprays of dill to soften the effect. Follow this with a single yellow yarrow, a cluster of chili peppers, and sprigs of fruiting ivy. Keep turning the string as you work so the material is bound on in a spiral to create an all-around display.

5 At this stage, bind in the next sunflower. These large flowerheads, like the yellow yarrow, are bold enough to stand on their own in the display and do not need to be added in groups like the more delicate plant material.

6 Follow the single
sunflower with sprigs of dill,
chili peppers, a single pincushion
protea, another sunflower, and yellow
yarrow. Keep making sure the flowers and
foliage are packed together and are arranged
in a spiral so that the string is covered.

7 Continue with the following sequence: sprays
of dill; chili peppers; fruiting ivy; pincushion protea;
sunflower; fruiting ivy; chili peppers; yellow yarrow;
sunflower. Start the sequence again from step 3 and
continue binding on material until you are 12 inches
(30 cm) from the end of the string.

8 The finished garland will be very
heavy, so attach it to the spokes of the
parasol section by section, using lengths
of string. If necessary, you can also stitch
the garland to the parasol fabric halfway
between each spoke. Spray-mist the
garland with water to keep it fresh.

45

# christmas wreath

Extend a warm welcome to guests during the festive season by decorating the front door with a Christmas wreath. The custom of bringing greenery into the home dates back to pagan times, when evergreen was brought inside for the winter solstice. Here, soft branches of blue fir entwined with shimmering gold ribbon, small cones, and clusters of cinnamon sticks and dried orange slices release a heady mix of spicy and fir-scented aromas.

**MATERIALS & EQUIPMENT**

circular wire frame, 17-inch (42.5-cm) diameter

sphagnum moss

plastic bag

5 branches blue fir (*Abies nobilis*)

gold cherub

6 dried orange slices

6 pine cones

24 cinnamon sticks, 6 groups of 4

¾ yard (60 cm) blue ribbon, ⅝ inch (1.5 cm) wide

2¾ yards (2.5 m) gold ribbon, 2 inches (5 cm) wide

spool wire • wire cutters • floral scissors • U-pins

medium-gauge floral wires • heavy-gauge floral wires

LEFT Roses and sprigs of skimmia make a perfect scented hanging ball for a special party or wedding. Make the ball by cutting a block of wet floral foam to shape. Attach a cord around the center of the foam and insert the skimmia and roses. Handle the rose heads with care to avoid bruising the petals.

BELOW Sweet-scented stephanotis has been wound around a circle to produce a dainty bridesmaid's ring.

BOTTOM OF PAGE Fragrant herbs and flowers are wired onto a small bridesmaid's basket filled with candy to offer to guests.

OPPOSITE, TOP OF PAGE Richly scented blue hyacinth bulbs are planted in a wire frame that has been filled with soil and covered with carpet moss to hold moisture within the wreath.

# scented wreaths

Bringing flowers, leaves, roots, and bark into the home to fill each room with fragrance has always been popular; the original scented wreath for the home may have been a circle of bay leaves, sacred to the Greek god Apollo. Choose flowers and foliage to grow in the yard for their fragrance as well as their appearance and carefully select the plant materials you bring indoors. Silver foliage plants such as blue fir or eucalyptus, with their fresh woody scent, work well, as do richly fragrant flowers such as hyacinths, stephanotis, roses, and lilies, whose heady scents will linger in the room.

ABOVE A wire frame that is shaped like a star has been covered with moss and sprigs of fragrant blue fir to create a welcoming Christmas wreath.

LEFT Silver-gray eucalyptus pods are bound to a circular frame using spool wire. The fragrance of the buds can be very strong, so the wreath is best hung outside so as not to be overpowering.

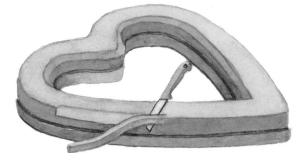

**1** Soak the heart-shaped foam base in water for five minutes. Then, using a floral knife, trim away a strip of foam about 1 inch (2.5 cm) wide on both the inner and outer edges; this will make the base more three-dimensional.

**2** To hang the display, tie the velvet ribbon around the top of the heart base and fasten it in place with a double knot. To prevent the ribbon from slipping, bend a heavy-gauge floral wire into a U-shape and insert it into the foam; it should straddle the ribbon, pinning it in place.

**3** Using floral scissors, trim the stems of the roses to within about 2 inches (5 cm) of the rose heads. Arrange the roses around the heart shape, inserting the stems so the flowers face alternately to the right and left.

**4** When you have laid the foundation of pink roses, fill in the heart with guelder rose. Cut down the stems to 2 inches (5 cm) and insert the guelder rose flowerets around the roses on the inner and outer edges.

**5** Divide each hydrangea flower into two or three groups of flowerets. Finish off the display by filling in any remaining exposed areas of foam on the heart shape with small groups of these delicate white flowers.

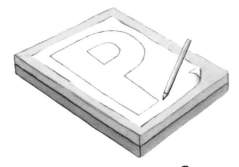

**1** Draw a paper template for the letter about 16 inches (40 cm) tall and 10 inches (25 cm) wide at the widest point. This scale will ensure the letter board is strong and thick enough to carry the gardenia flowers.

**2** Using a floral knife, score around the edge of the letter—here a P—to transfer the design to the board. Cut out the shape using the scored line as a guide.

**3** Place the square pot, the gravel, the pole, the P-shaped board (face down), the clematis vine, and some clematis twigs on a sheet of scrap paper. Spray the items gold and leave to dry.

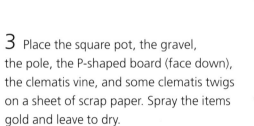

**4** Soak the P-shape in water for ten minutes and then push about 10 inches (25 cm) of the pole into the base of the letter. If necessary, bind the pole and designer board together with floral tape to make it secure.

**5** Bend one gold-sprayed vine around the outline of the letter. Cut lengths of medium-gauge floral wire about 3 inches (8 cm) long and bend them into hairpins. Pin the vine in place around the letter.

**6** Cut sprigs of flowers and foliage about 2 inches (5 cm) long, but reserve all the flowering stems for the top surface of the P-shape. Insert the leaf stems into the board around the sides of the P-shape. Use shorter leaf stems for the inner edge of the central hole.

**7** When all the edges are covered in leaves, add sprigs of gardenia flowers to the top edge of the letter. Trim the stem of each flowering sprig to about 1 inch (2.5 cm) and strip away a few of the lower leaves. Insert each of the flower sprigs, butting them up close to one another around the board.

**8** To visually soften the P-shaped outline, add a handful of gold twigs to the edge of the display. Make sure the twigs face in different directions so they look natural.

**9** Last, partly fill the pot with large pebbles to weigh it down. Insert the letter on its pole and, when it is straight, add the rest of the stones. Sprinkle a layer of gold gravel on top. To finish, twist a length of gold-sprayed clematis vine around the pole and display the finished letter face out.

# wreath of lilies and apples

I enjoy using fruit and flowers together, and here, crisp green apples and beautiful scented white lilies offer a fresh lime-green mix of plant material. The white lilies sit on presoaked floral foam blocks, but even so, be warned that the display will have a limited life, because the wired apples release a natural gas that ages plant material.

**MATERIALS & EQUIPMENT**

circular honeysuckle vine wreath, 22-inch (55-cm) diameter

carpet moss

3 small dome-shaped blocks of floral foam with screw-in bases

18 green apples

9 sprigs fruiting ivy (*Hedera*)

3 white hydrangeas (*Hydrangea*)

2 pure white lilies (*Lilium* 'Casa Blanca')

6 white lilies with creamy yellow centers (*Lilium* 'Pompeii')

3 strands trailing ivy (*Hedera*), 8–12 inches (20–30 cm) long

medium-gauge floral wires • floral scissors

1  Divide the damp carpet moss into three clumps, approximately 4 inches (10 cm) long. Arrange the clumps an equal distance apart at three points on the wreath. This flat, damp moss does not need to be glued into place; simply tuck the corners of each clump of moss under the vine binding on the wreath base.

2  Next, soak the three floral foam domes in water for five minutes. Position each one on the wreath between the moss, and screw their coiled bases through the open-weave base. To hold the domes in place, thread medium-gauge floral wires through them on both sides. Bend each wire into a hairpin and push the ends through the wreath and back on themselves.

3  To wire the apples, push a length of medium-gauge floral wire through the bottom third of each fruit. Twist one leg of wire around the other and bring them together. Place three apples on each clump of moss and three around each dome. Push the floral wires through the wreath base and bind them around the vine at the back of the wreath.

4  To keep the flowers and foliage alive as long as possible, arrange them on the presoaked foam domes. Begin with the fruiting ivy foliage. Trim the sprays to 2 inches (5 cm) and remove the lower leaves. Insert two or three sprigs of fruiting ivy into each of the three domes.

5 Continue by adding the hydrangea heads. Trim their woody stems to 1 inch (2.5 cm) and strip them of leaves. Insert one hydrangea into each of the three foam domes. Place the flowers on the lower edges of the foam and for added interest make sure one sits on the inner edge of the wreath and two sit on the outer edge.

6 Continue by trimming all eight lily stems to 1 inch (2.5 cm) and stripping the stems of any leaves. Insert the two 'Casa Blanca' lilies into one of the floral foam domes and insert three 'Pompeii' lilies into each of the other two domes.

7 Last, weave two or three lengths of trailing ivy, about 8–12 inches (20–30 cm) long, between the fresh flowers and foliage to soften the overall effect. Insert the end of each trailing ivy strand into a floral foam dome to keep it alive. Hang the finished display from a nail. Spray-mist the moss and the three domes daily to keep them moist.

**OPPOSITE TOP** Small apples are wired to a moss frame by threading a floral wire through the apple flesh and twisting the ends together. Leaves and skimmia flowers help to conceal the moss.

**OPPOSITE BELOW LEFT** Red ornamental chili peppers are wired onto a single-wire wreath frame. Arrange the stalks end-to-end for variety and pack them tightly to conceal the wire base.

**OPPOSITE BELOW RIGHT** Store garlic in the kitchen by attaching raffia to the stalk of each garlic bulb and threading the bulbs onto a twig frame. Garlic cloves can be cut off as required for use in cooking.

**LEFT** Flowers and foliage can be used to decorate baskets of food for a party. Here, ivy and poppies are threaded through a twig basket filled with dried fruit and nuts. Wash foliage carefully when using it to decorate food.

**ABOVE** Children of all ages will love this, although they may not leave it alone. Cover a star-shaped wire frame with ½-inch (1-cm) chicken wire, tie it onto a pole, and cement it into a pot. Spray the star gold and leave it to dry while you tie ribbons onto candy wrappers. Then attach the candy to the wire to cover the star. Hide the cement with candy, too.

**ABOVE** Terracotta pots filled with herbs and tied together with rope make a decorative roof-top or terrace display for the urban gardener.

**RIGHT** For a summery look, make and hang a garland of flowers around a table. Choose a strong-headed flower such as marguerite daisies and thread the back of each flowerhead onto some spool wire.

# culinary themes

Foods, particularly breads, have long been associated with wreaths. The Egyptians fashioned bread into rings as a form of payment before the introduction of money, while in Greece, the family makes a circular wedding bread to symbolize well-being and good fortune. Above all, culinary wreaths are a useful and attractive way to store ingredients such as chili peppers, garlic, and candy, while food baskets and dessert tables look wonderful draped in flowers and foliage.

1 Dampen the sphagnum moss and tease it out to remove any loose leaves or bark. Take a large clump of moss and spread it along the frame. Secure the moss in place by binding it with spool wire. Continue adding moss and wiring it tightly to the frame until the circle is covered.

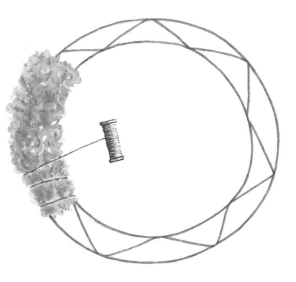

2 To prevent the damp moss wreath from leaking, line the back of the frame with plastic. To do this, cut a plastic bag into 4-inch (10-cm) strips. Fasten a strip of plastic to the edge of the wreath with a U-pin. Fold the plastic in a zigzag, pinning as you go, so that it follows the frame. Make sure that you cover the whole circle in this way.

3 Wire up each lemon, lime, and orange as follows: take a medium-gauge floral wire and push one end through the bottom quarter of the fruit. Bring the ends of the wire together and twist them around each other. Repeat until all the fruits are wired up.

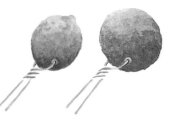

4 Begin attaching the lemons to the wreath. Push the ends of the floral wire through the moss and then bend them back and tuck them into the underside of the wreath to anchor the fruit. Attach three groups of five lemons in this way, arranging the groups an equal distance from one another.

**5** Using the same technique as described in step 4, add three groups of wired oranges and three groups of wired limes to the wreath.

**6** Cut the fruiting ivy sprigs to 6 inches (15 cm) and make up small bunches of three to five stems. To wire the bunches, bend a medium-gauge floral wire into a hairpin shape with one leg longer than the other. Hold the U-end against the stems and wrap the long leg of wire around the stems and the other leg of wire, then bring the wires together. Wire up at least 80 sprays.

**7** Lastly, add the delicate sprays of fruiting ivy to the display. Use the foliage to fill in any gaps between the citrus fruits and to cover up any areas of moss on the wreath that are still exposed.

# grape and cherry garland

For summer buffets, a garland of fruit and edible nasturtium flowers around the
dessert table makes a fresh and colorful addition. Dainty garlands such as this
can be simply constructed on a thin gold cord and pinned to the tablecloth.
First wash the materials, especially nasturtiums, to make sure they are bug free.

**MATERIALS & EQUIPMENT**

the length of rope and quantity of fruit, nasturtiums, and ivy will depend
on the size of your chosen table; for a table 24 inches (60 cm) in diameter allow:

2¾ yards (2.5 m) gold cord, ½-inch (1-cm) diameter

5 strands of trailing ivy (*Hedera*), 20 inches (50 cm) long

2½ pounds (1 kg) green and black grapes

2½ pounds (1 kg) cherries

6 packs edible nasturtiums (*Tropaeolum*)

floral scissors • floral tape

pearl-headed pins • medium-gauge floral wires

1 Figure out exactly how much gold cord you need to make the garland by taking the cord around the table edge. Cut the cord to length and then start the garland by twisting a strand of trailing ivy around the gold cord.

2 Bind the first stem end of ivy to the gold cord with floral tape. This will hold the stem in place and seal it, preventing it from drying out. Use floral tape to join more strands of ivy to one another and to bind them to the gold cord.

3 When you have woven ivy along the length of gold cord and bound the ends with floral tape, using the pearl-headed pins, attach the cord securely to the edge of the tablecloth so it can carry the weight of the fruit and flowers without sagging. Make sure the pinheads are visible at the top edge. Work your way around the table, pinning the cord to the cloth at 8-inch (20-cm) intervals.

4 Next, wire bunches of grapes and cherries on double-leg mounts using medium-gauge floral wires. To do this, bend a wire into a U-shape, creating a long and a short end. Place the shorter end of wire against the fruit stems and wrap the longer leg of wire around the stems three times. Then bring the two ends together.

5 Attach bunches of grapes to the garland at 8-inch (20-cm) intervals. Thread the floral wires through the cord from the top edge of the table. Twist the wires around the cord and then flop the bunches of grapes over so they hang down. Then hide the floral wires by carefully repositioning the ivy leaves. Try to alternate between bunches of black and green grapes.

6 When you have wired the bunches of grapes around the entire garland, begin attaching groups of cherries. Use the same technique as described in step 5, but place the cherries between the bunches of grapes. Again, cover the wires under ivy leaves.

7 When all the cherries are secure, finish the garland with nasturtium flowers. Trim the flower stems to 2 inches (5 cm); simply tuck each thin, curved stem behind the gold cord and it will stay in place. Tuck the flowers behind the cord from both the top and bottom edge; this way the flowers will all face in different directions.

# eggplant and orchid wreath

The striking contrast of deep burgundy eggplant and anthuriums set against vivid yellow pattypan squashes and yarrow produces a richly exotic table display. The flowers and foliage are grouped together for maximum visual impact and interwoven with swirls of stephanandra stems to create movement.

### MATERIALS & EQUIPMENT

circular wire frame, 18-inch (45-cm) diameter

sphagnum moss

9 anthuriums (*Anthurium*)

30 baby eggplants

2 stems stephanandra vine (*Stephanandra tanakae*), 3 feet (1 m) long,
leaves removed and reserved

10 sprays yellow yarrow (*Achillea* 'Moonshine')

15 orchids (*Cymbidium*) • 30 yellow pattypan squash

spool wire • wire cutters • floral scissors

U-pins • heavy-gauge floral wires • medium-gauge floral wires

1 Cover the wire frame with clumps of damp moss. As you place the moss on the base, wind spool wire tightly around it to secure the moss to the frame. Next, using floral scissors, trim away any straggly pieces so the moss sits neatly against the circular wire frame.

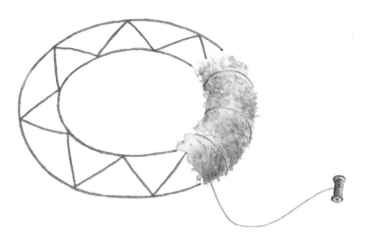

2 Soak the anthuriums in water and flower food to condition them and then cut the stems to 4 inches (10 cm). Wire the flowers using a medium-gauge floral wire bent into a hairpin shape with one leg longer than the other. Hold the U-end against a stem. Wrap the long leg of wire around the stem and the other leg, then pull the two ends together. Insert three groups of two flowers equidistant from one another on the wreath. Place each pair back to back.

3 Build up the rest of the display around the anthuriums. Wire each eggplant by threading a heavy-gauge floral wire through the skin and then twisting the two ends together. Arrange ten eggplants in a fan shape around the anthuriums. To secure the eggplants, push the wires into the moss and turn each wire back on itself.

4 Next, wire each stephanandra leaf and each stem of yellow yarrow. Use a double-leg mount as described in step 2. Fill any spaces between the flowers and eggplants with the leaves. Then, working out from the three groups of flowers and vegetables, fill in the wreath base with sprays of yellow yarrow.

5 Insert a wired anthurium next to the yarrow on the outer edge. Next, wire each orchid head on a medium-gauge floral wire using a double-leg mount as described in step 2. Arrange half the orchids in tight groups on the inner edge of the wreath.

6 Fill in space between the orchid heads and the eggplant groups with pattypan squash. Wire these vegetables as you would eggplants (see step 3), and then insert three groups of ten pattypans each into the moss equidistant from one another. Add the rest of the wired orchids on the outer edge of the wreath to link the groups. Last, fill areas where moss is still visible with remaining stephanandra leaves.

7 Using medium-gauge floral wire, double-leg mount one end of a length of vine as described in step 2. Push the wires through the moss base of the wreath to hold the vine in place. Wrap the vine loosely around the flowers and vegetables in a series of decorative loops. To finish, double-leg mount the other end of the vine and push the wires into the base. Repeat this step for the second length of vine.

**ABOVE** A hand-tied posy adds the finishing touch to a church event. Soft green lady's mantle and pink hydrangeas are mixed with deep red peonies, cockscomb, and 'Black Velvet' roses. The flowers were threaded through an iron ring candle holder on the cross to hold them in place.

**ABOVE** Constructed from plant stakes held together with spool wire, this eye-catching gold star is covered in hundreds of tiny oak leaves. Each leaf has been dried, sprayed gold, and glued onto the stakes. Hide the framework by making sure that the gold oak leaves overlap one another.

**ABOVE** Ivy and butcher's-broom foliage are mixed with lilac, hyacinths, ranunculi, and bell-shaped campanula spires to produce a fragrant display. A fresh floral foam dome, which clips onto the arm of the church pew end, forms the foundation for this diamond-shaped arrangement.

# celebrations

Since ancient Greek and Roman times, people have chosen wreaths and garlands to celebrate great events. The Greeks crowned the winners of their poetic and athletic competitions with garlands of fresh laurel, oak, and olive leaves, while the Romans chose head wreaths to honor their great military heroes. What better way to mark a special occasion, whether it is Valentine's Day, Christmas, or an anniversary, than by following in this grand tradition and creating a memorable display of flowers or foliage?

**ABOVE** To create a token of your love on Valentine's Day, soften red dogwood stems by soaking them in warm water and bend them into a heart. Secure the shape with red ribbon and add two stems of beautiful 'Grand Prix' roses.
**RIGHT** A dazzling display for a golden wedding anniversary celebration has been created by packing a heart-shaped frame with damp moss and covering it in a background of soft lilac and pale green hydrangeas, topped with stunning yellow 'Sultan' gerberas and 'Golden Gate' roses.

ABOVE A spectacular Christmas wreath is created using a whorl of birch twigs dipped in red paint and sprinkled with glitter. To shape the birch twigs into a ring, cut the stems to 3 inches (7.5 cm) long and bind groups of birch twigs to one another with spool wire. Bend all of the twigs into a circle as you work until the ring is complete. Tiny lights are threaded through the birch at the back of the wreath to make the display sparkle, and the cord is hidden from view with more twigs if necessary.

LEFT A hanging festive wreath of bright flowers and candles is built up from a wire-frame foundation covered in moss. The candles and curls of ribbon are then attached to the base with heavy-gauge floral wires before the display is hung. Once in location, fruiting ivy and sea holly form a bed of foliage for vivid marigolds, 'Jaguar' roses, ranunculi, and anemones.

1 Condition the cut flowers and foliage in water for up to 12 hours. Meanwhile, create the wire framework for the headdress. Using silver wire, join two fine-gauge floral wires. Bind the length of wire in floral tape.

2 Using a large tin as a mold, bend the wire into a circle and check that it fits the wearer's head. Hook the ends to make a clasp.

3 Wire individual ivy leaves to use later to cover the hooks at the end of the headdress. To do this, stitch a fine-gauge floral wire through the midrib of each ivy leaf. Pull the wire ends down and twist them together. Bind the wire and leaf base with floral tape to seal in the leaf moisture and form a stem.

4 Next, wire delicate sprigs of ivy and lilies-of-the-valley for support. Cut each stem to 4 inches (10 cm) and wind a medium-gauge floral wire along its length, taking care to avoid the ivy leaves or lily-of-the-valley flowerets. Bind the wire with floral tape.

5 Next, wire the hyacinths. Cut off flowerets from the flower. Push a medium-gauge floral wire up through the base of the floweret, and make a hook. Pull the wire back down inside the floweret to anchor the hook. Thread a silver wire crosswise through the bottom third of the floweret. Pinch the wires together and bind with floral tape. Wire fritillaries and bachelor's buttons using this method.

6 Next, wire the fatter-stemmed lisianthus and ranunculi. To do this, cut off most of the stem, leaving ½ inch (1 cm). Push a medium-gauge floral wire up through the stem and flower until it reaches the calyx in the lower third of the flowerhead. Insert a silver wire crosswise through the stem, making one end longer than the other. Pinch the wires together and wind the longer length of silver wire around the stem. Bind with floral tape.

**7** Lay out the flowers and foliage on your work surface according to type; this makes wiring them onto the framework easier. Straighten the frame circle; hide the clasp by placing a wired ivy leaf against it. Bind the leaf with floral tape.

**8** Bind on more flowers and foliage with floral tape to build up the headdress. Add lilies-of-the-valley followed by bachelor's buttons, ranunculi, ivy sprigs, hyacinth flowerets, and lisianthus. Add the smaller flowers in groups so they can be seen and larger flowers in twos or threes. Trim the stems as you work.

**9** After the lisianthus, bind in ivy leaves, then fritillaries; then begin the sequence again from step 8. Let the stems overlap so the headdress looks full. Last, cover the second part of the clasp in an ivy leaf as described in step 7. To finish, bind the tape around the wire and cut.

**10** Finally, bend the wreath back into a circle. Spray-mist the wreath with water to keep it fresh and pinch the clasp together with pliers to hold the headdress in place.

# heart-shaped table centerpiece

Tall displays of flowers and foliage, either incorporated on
a candelabra or, as here, elevated on a pole, have become
increasingly fashionable for the guest tables at weddings. Not
only do they make a theatrical impact in a large room, they allow
guests to witness the speeches without anything obstructing their view.

### MATERIALS & EQUIPMENT

stone urn, 18 inches (45 cm) high, 12-inch (30-cm) diameter

2 blocks floral foam, 8 x 4 x 3 inches (20 x 10 x 8 cm)

heart-shaped twig wreath, 10 inches (25 cm) across at widest point • sphagnum moss

1-inch (2.5 cm) chicken wire, 1 x 3 feet (25 x 100 cm) • wooden pole, 32 inches (80 cm) long

15 sprigs beech foliage (*Fagus*) • 15 sprigs lady's mantle (*Alchemilla mollis*)

15 sprigs pittosporum (*Pittosporum*) • 15 sprigs guelder rose (*Viburnum opulus*)

13 mauve hydrangeas (*Hydrangea*) • 14 blue scabious (*Scabiosa*)

16 pink lisianthus (*Eustoma grandiflorum*) • 15 pale pink roses (*Rosa* 'Delilah')

strand of ivy (*Hedera*), approximately 30 inches (75 cm) long

plastic bag • floral knife • floral tape • floral scissors

wire cutters • spool wire • heavy-gauge floral wire

1 Line the urn with a plastic bag and then wedge two presoaked blocks of floral foam into it. For a good fit, use a floral knife to trim down the two sides of the foam blocks.

2 Tape the wet foam blocks into place using waterproof floral tape. Next, trim the top edge of the plastic bag so it sits neatly inside the rim.

3 Working from the outer edges of the urn to the center, build up a mound shape of foliage using sprigs of beech, lady's mantle, pittosporum, and guelder rose. For the outer edges, cut 10-inch (25-cm) sprigs and insert them upside-down so they trail over the edges. Use shorter lengths of foliage as you fill in the center.

4 When the foam is covered with foliage, add the flowers, starting with five hydrangea heads. Cut the flower stems to 8 inches (20 cm) and, following the mound shape of foliage, distribute the shapes and colors of the flowers evenly, as the display will be viewed from all sides.

5 To make the heart-shaped frame, lay the chicken wire on a flat surface and place the twig wreath on top. Fill the frame with presoaked moss and then fold the wire over the heart to sandwich the moss in place.

6 Cut and mold the chicken wire around the heart-shaped base. Using spool wire, fasten the edges of the chicken wire together securely. Next, push about 4 inches (10 cm) of the pole through the base of the twig heart. Secure the pole to the heart frame with a heavy-gauge floral wire. To do this, thread the wire through the twig frame and tie it around the pole.

7 Cover both faces of the heart and the edges with sprigs of foliage as used for the urn. Cut the stems to 2 inches (5 cm) long and, working from the outer edges to the center, push the stems directly into the moss.

8 Continue by adding the flowers. Start with hydrangeas, as for the urn. Cut all the flower stems to about 1½ inches (3 cm) long and distribute their shapes and colors evenly across both sides of the heart.

9 When the heart is complete, insert the pole into the floral foam in the center of the urn. Wrap one end of the strand of ivy around the chicken wire at the base of the heart to hold it in place, and then wind the ivy down the length of the pole to finish.

# chair-back decoration

This simple hand-tied swag of scented pink roses and rich purple lisianthus is easy to make and looks stunning. Use a generous length of brightly colored satin ribbon to attach the swag flamboyantly to the back of the chair where a guest of honor will sit, or make several to decorate the aisle seats at a wedding.

### MATERIALS & EQUIPMENT

1 yard (1 m) raffia

5 stems viburnum (*Viburnum tinus*)

16 deep pink roses (*Rosa* 'Martinez')

9 pale pink roses (*Rosa* 'Delilah')

4 cockscomb (*Celosia argentea*)

18 purple lisianthus (*Eustoma grandiflorum*)

4 yards (3.5 m) cerise ribbon, 2 inches (5 cm) wide

floral scissors

1 Cut the viburnum stems to 16 inches (40 cm). To form the foundation of this display, hold one stem of foliage upright and then crisscross another stem behind (to the right) and a third in front (to the left). Bind the stems with raffia.

2 Add two more viburnum stems, crisscrossing one behind and one in front. Pull the stems down into the display to fill in any gaps; remember that you are trying to create a diamond shape. When the viburnum stems are in place, bind them into the bunch with raffia. Trim the stems to 8 inches (20 cm).

3 Next add the 'Martinez' roses. Take three stems about 24 inches (60 cm) long and arrange them behind the viburnum. Stand one rose in the center and tilt one to the left and one to the right. Tie the roses to the viburnum at the center point with raffia.

4 Continue building up the tied bunch by adding two more 'Martinez' roses. Thread the stems at an angle through the viburnum and pull the rose heads down into the display to fill in the diamond shape. Tie the rose stems with raffia and trim them to the same length as the viburnum stems.

5 Continue weaving and binding the 'Martinez' roses into the bouquet, crisscrossing the flowers through the tied bunch to obtain an even distribution of color. Next, add the 'Delilah' roses using the same crisscross technique. Trim the stems to one length.

6 Next, add the cockscomb stems to fill any obvious gaps between the roses and viburnum. Last, add long stems of purple lisianthus to the front and back of the bouquet. Tie the flower stems in place with raffia and trim down the lisianthus and cockscomb stems to the same length as the roses and viburnum.

7 To make the bow, cut two pieces of ribbon 20 inches (50 cm) long. Fold one piece into three loops and pinch the loops together in the middle. Take the second ribbon and tie it in a single knot around the center of the loops.

8 Last, tie the bouquet to the back of the chair with a 2-yard (2.5-m) length of ribbon. When it is secure, fasten the bow on the bouquet using the bow's short ribbon tails.

# banister garland

Create a grand staircase for your guests by constructing an abundant garland
of fresh flowers and foliage on a floral foam base. The foam foundation
can be bought in standard lengths from specialized florists and joined
together to achieve the desired length. Presoak the foam base to keep the
fresh materials well watered, and take care to fasten the garland securely
to the banister, since the finished display will be very heavy.

## MATERIALS & EQUIPMENT

floral foam garland, available in 6-foot (2-m) lengths composed of 6-inch (15-cm) sections;
for each 6-inch (15-cm) section you will need approximately:

20 sprigs dusty miller (*Senecio cineraria*)

4 green double lisianthus (*Eustoma grandiflorum*)

4 pink double lisianthus (*Eustoma grandiflorum*)

2 white tuberoses (*Polianthes tuberosa*)

2–3 cream roses (*Rosa* 'Anna')

10 sprigs snowberry (*Symphoricarpos*)

1 yard (1 m) satin ribbon, 1¾ inches (4 cm) wide

plastic sheets • floral scissors

spool wire • wire cutters

**1** Soak each section of the foam garland in water for five minutes. Meanwhile, cover the stairs with plastic sheets. Then, protect the wooden handrail. To do this, bind lengths of ribbon around the rail at the points where you intend to attach the garland. Using spool wire, bind the presoaked garland to the handrail on top of the protective ribbon. Secure every sixth section of foam using this technique.

**2** Cut 12 sprigs of dusty miller 8 inches (20 cm) long and strip off the lower leaves. Use four sprigs to hide the ribbon and wire that attach the garland to the rail. Insert eight sprigs around the edges of the first section of foam to conceal the back of the display. Next, prepare shorter, 6-inch (15-cm) lengths of foliage, stripping off the lower 2 inches (5 cm) of leaves. Insert about eight sprigs into the foam surface until it is covered. Repeat this technique to cover the seams and each of the foam sections.

**3** Next, trim the stems of the green and pink double lisianthus to 7 inches (18 cm). Arrange four green lisianthus in a zigzag on the first section of foam and then space four pink lisianthus in between. Repeat this step for each section of the garland.

4 Trim the white tuberose stems to 8 inches (20 cm). Insert two stems into each section of foam, one near the top and the other at the center. Weave the rest of the flowers through the display following the garland shape.

5 Cut the cream rose stems to 8 inches (20 cm), snipping the ends at a 45° angle to create a larger surface area to take up water. Insert two or three roses per section, placing them pointing up, down, or to the sides of the foam, but always following the curved shape of the display.

6 Last, trim lengths of snowberry to 10 inches (25 cm). Insert about five sprigs at the top and bottom edge of each section so the berries trail and soften the effect of this flower garland.

# wreath materials

Wreath frames can be purchased from good florists, garden centers, and specialized floristry suppliers, and are available in an extraordinary variety of shapes and sizes. Made from natural materials such as flexible dogwood stems, honeysuckle, or clematis vine, and bound together with spool wire or garden string, these simple rigid foundations form the building blocks of fresh or dried flower displays.

A purchased wreath base is always a worthwhile investment because, unlike fresh floral foam bases, they can be reused again and again. However, if you want to create a particular shape it may be simpler and more cost-effective to create your own base. Amateur gardeners or enthusiastic walkers can collect plant stems and trailing vines from the yard or countryside to fashion into wreath bases. Select any pliable woody stems and try to harvest these branches in spring before the sap rises, or in the

fall after the sap has fallen. Dogwood, corkscrew hazel, and birch are my favorite woods, and honeysuckle, kiwi, wisteria, and grape are my favorite garden vines, but you can also find clematis and honeysuckle in the wild. If the twigs or vines are dry, soak them in warm water until they become more flexible and easier to work with. Start by picking out a few long stems and gently ease them into a circle. If the stems are too short, keep adding new lengths by staggering and overlapping stems until you have a circle. Bind the stems tightly with spool wire as you work to keep the twigs in place. The wire can be removed when the stems are dry, if they have taken on the right shape.

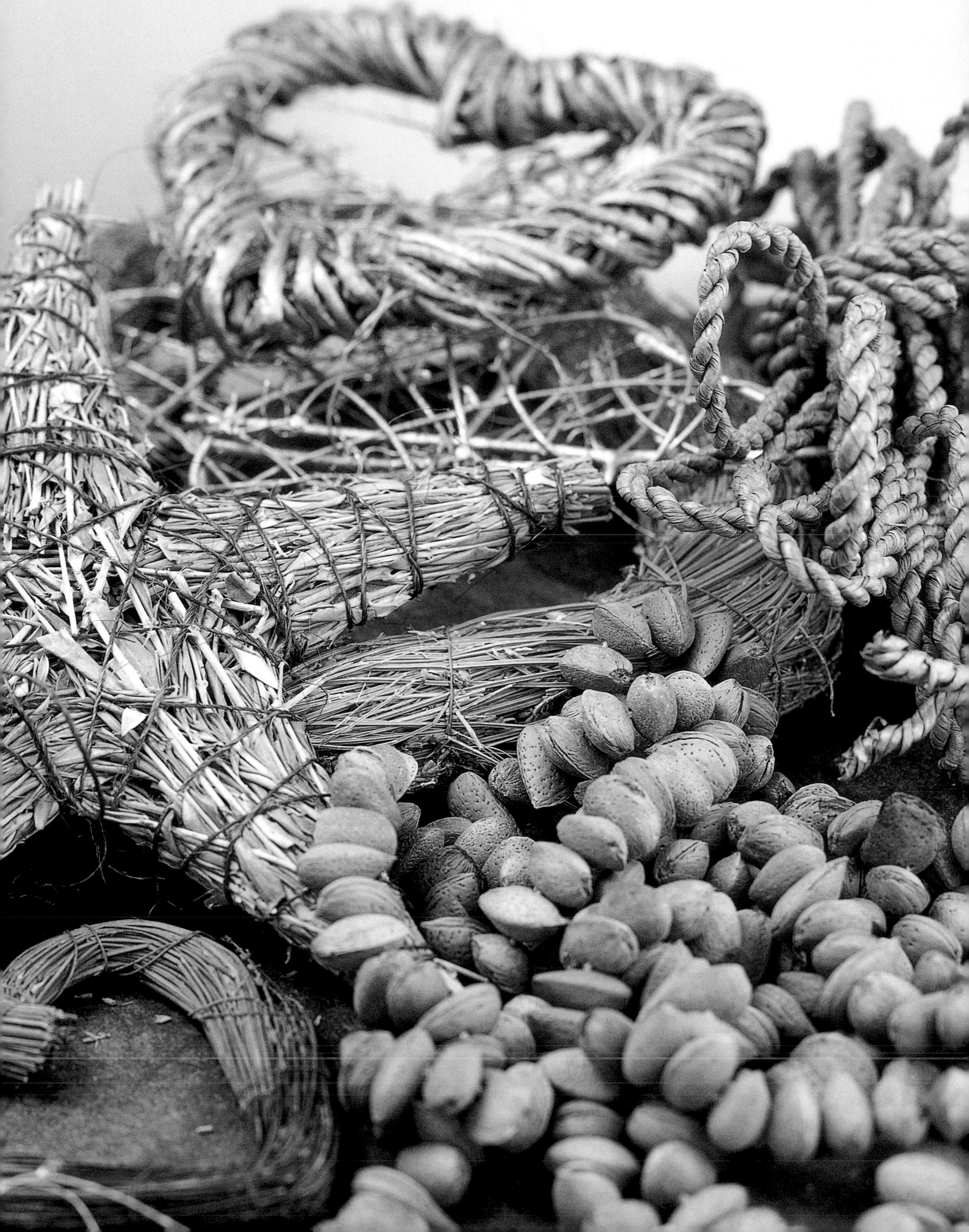

## WIRE FRAMES

Rigid wire wreath frames can be purchased ready-made in a bewildering number of dimensions. There is little standardization for popular shapes, such as crosses, circles, and stars, since manufacturers from different countries have their own sizing systems based largely around funeral wreath traditions.

If you cannot buy the size or shape of frame you require, you could try making your own, but bear in mind that it may be difficult to buy materials such as floral wires, spool wire, and other sundries in small quantities.

Most florists will carry a limited stock, but they may be reluctant to sell them to the public, and they may have to order them specially from wholesalers. For a more "do-it-yourself" approach, try molding wire coat hangers into simple heart-shaped frames or folding a length of chicken wire around a strip of damp moss and bending it into a shape. Medium-gauge floral wires and silver wire form the underlying structure for lightweight bridal headdresses, but for more sturdy metal-framed structures, you could commission a metal worker to solder iron into the shapes that you required.

Wire frames are more permanent than either twig or foam bases and can be used again and again. Often damp moss is attached to the bare wire frame with spool wire to form a moist bed for fresh flowers. If the moss is very damp, the back of the wire wreath can be lined with plastic to protect the surface.

## LARGE-SCALE DESIGNS

Wire frames are ideally suited to particularly large and heavy displays. For grand-scale designs, two wire frames can be bound together with spool wire to reinforce the structure; sturdy wire frames are used to support a large nautical-theme wreath constructed out of twists of rope and shells (see page 12) as well as a heavy frame of driftwood (see page 28).

**FLORAL FOAM BASES**

Fresh floral foam is green, and dry foam is either brown or gray. Both types of foam come in blocks or specially molded shapes; fresh foam is soaked in water before use to prolong the life of the flowers and foliage. Inserting stems into moist foam will help plant materials stay fresh for longer, although they will not last as long as they would if arranged in a vase of water. Although fresh floral foam bases are simple to work with, they are really suitable only for short-term hanging decorations, because as the foam dries out and contracts, the plant material becomes dislodged and drops out. For this reason, foam shapes are best used for table centerpieces; the foam sits in a plastic base that protects the table surface. When soaking a fresh floral foam block in water, allow the foam to sink gradually. When air bubbles no longer rise to the surface, it is ready for use. Bear in mind that fresh foam can be used for only one fresh-flower display, since it will not take up water effectively after it has had its first soak.

Although there are only a few floral foam manufacturers, the styles and shapes of the products they offer vary enormously. By ordering supplies from mail-order catalogs, you can select the sizes and dimensions you wish, as good florists and garden centers hold only limited stock. In addition to round ring frames, balls, cones, and open-heart shapes, there are flat designer boards that can be cut into any shape. Also, specialized foam designs can be purchased for keeping fresh flowers and foliage alive on twig and wire wreaths. One type consists of a small block of dome-shaped floral foam held in a plastic cage with a screw-in base. Another type, designed to attach fresh flower displays to church pews, consists of a similar dome with a removable attachment that clips onto the pew end.

**FLEXIBLE BASES**

Flexible foam bases, which can be draped along a banister, are also available for creating garlands out of delicate plant materials that require a constant supply of water to prevent them from wilting. These specially manufactured floral foam bases can be bought in 6-foot (2-m) lengths, divided into sections, and must be soaked well in water before use.

# equipment & techniques

## WREATH-MAKING EQUIPMENT

A flat, non-scratch work surface that stands at a suitable height so the user does not have to stoop is the first piece of equipment needed for wreath-making. It is also useful when you are creating hanging wreaths to have a place where you can hang the display so you can check how the finished arrangement will look. Scrap paper on the work surface and drop cloths on the floor are also essential, especially when you are working on a display on location. Opt for plastic rather than fabric drop cloths to prevent moisture from seeping through to the floor or carpet below. When you have finished, you can simply fold up the ground sheets to clear away any waste material.

## ESSENTIAL TOOLS

Floristry scissors and shears are essential for collecting fresh plant materials and cutting stems. A small floral knife is handy for stripping the lower leaves from stems and for trimming blocks of floral foam to shape. Wire cutters are required for cutting chicken wire and floral wires, and pliers are useful for closing up clasps on headdresses. A glue gun is an indispensable tool for those who enjoy attaching unusual and heavy items, such as shells and wood, to wreaths, but should be used with care. The hot liquid glue adheres most materials, including wet items and dry porous objects, and it saves time, as it takes only a few seconds for the glue to dry. Both high- and low-temperature guns are available; low-temperature guns are more suitable for attaching fresh plant material, which can scorch on exposure to heat. Waterproof floral tape is also useful for anchoring wet foam blocks in containers, as is gutta-percha tape, which seals moisture within plant stems.

## CONDITIONING PLANTS

The most recent research recommends the following simple guidelines for conditioning fresh flowers and foliage before they are arranged on a

wreath. If you follow these measures and condition flowers and foliage for several hours or overnight, they will last longer in the finished display. As a general rule, take at least 1¼ inches (3 cm) off the bottom of the stem and make a slanted cut with a sharp floral knife to expose the maximum surface area to water, rather than smashing or splitting the base of the stem. Next, remove the lower leaves from the plant stems, because leaves submerged under water may rot and produce bacteria that will shorten the life of the plant material. Before placing the cut flowers and foliage in a container for conditioning, make sure that it is scrupulously clean and fill it with fresh lukewarm water, mixed with flower food. The food will feed the flowers, promoting longer life, and will prevent bacteria from growing.

## PROTECTING SURFACES

It is a good idea to protect doors, walls, and tables, or any other surfaces or items of furniture in the home that may come into contact with water or moisture from fresh flower wreaths or garlands. Water is particularly harmful to unprotected wood finishes and can leave marks that are difficult to remove or cause the wood to warp. For small table wreaths, simply place a waterproof table mat or piece of thick felt under the tablecloth, but for grand-scale designs that are too large to sit on a mat, you will have to make your own protective covering out of a waterproof material. The best method is to cut up a plastic bag into long thin strips and fasten the strips to the back of the wreath with U-pins to prevent dampness from penetrating the furniture or wall.

Pin several strips of plastic over the damp moss covering the wreath base to prevent any water seepage.

To make a solid double-sided heart-shaped base for fresh flowers, fill the center of an open-heart-shaped twig wreath with damp moss or presoaked floral foam blocks; then wrap it in a sheet of chicken wire and fasten the edges with lengths of spool wire.

### DRYING YOUR OWN MATERIALS

If you wish to create more permanent wreaths, buy bunches of dried materials, such as roses and glycerinated beech leaves, from a good florist, or try harvesting and drying your own materials, such as roses from the yard. In recent years, there have been great improvements in the quality of dried flowers available for purchase, mainly due to new techniques for freeze-drying flowerheads, particularly roses. These new methods have produced amazingly lifelike flowers whose petals maintain their natural beauty and suppleness. However, displays using freeze-dried flowers must be kept away from moist conditions, such as those found in kitchens and bathrooms, because the flowers tend to absorb moisture from the air and deteriorate rapidly.

The simplest way to dry your own plant materials for wreath-making is to hang them in bunches and store them in a cool, dark, dry room. If you have a warm, dry closet with enough space, use it as a drying area. Warm air will dry plant materials

Two standard blocks of floral foam are used to make a base for fresh flowers and foliage in a stone urn. The urn is lined with plastic before the presoaked blocks are added, their edges tapered to shape with a floral knife.

quickly, with only a small amount of color fading. When the materials are thoroughly dry, store them in large cardboard boxes or paper bags. Make sure that the flowers or leaves do not touch one another and place them between layers of tissue paper to avoid damaging the plant material. Avoid using plastic bags, as they become moist and cause the dried flowers and leaves to deteriorate.

### ADAPTING WREATH BASES

If you cannot find the exact wreath base you need for your project, adapt the materials you have at your disposal and make your own. For example, if you want to create a heart of fresh flowers, fill an existing heart-shaped twig frame with damp moss or blocks of presoaked floral foam and sandwich the moss or foam within the frame with chicken wire. Remember, most materials can be cut or trimmed to shape to suit your needs. For example, presoaked floral foam can be tapered to fit any

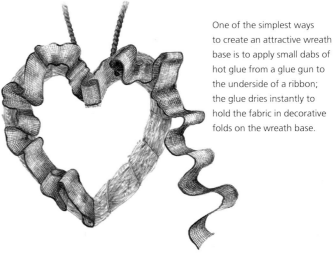

One of the simplest ways to create an attractive wreath base is to apply small dabs of hot glue from a glue gun to the underside of a ribbon; the glue dries instantly to hold the fabric in decorative folds on the wreath base.

container and then held in place with waterproof floral tape, and flat designer board can be cut into a letter or number, using a template as a guide. Twig and dry foam bases are even more versatile than floral foam and form the foundation for many displays; they can be used time and again to create a different effect each time. A twig frame makes a good starting point for a fabric wreath—wrap the frame in quilted material to create a padded effect, then cover it in the fabric of your choice. Alternatively, natural wreath bases can be customized by coating them with different colored spray paint.

### ATTACHING MATERIALS TO WREATH BASES

The stems of fresh flowers and foliage are easy to insert in a fresh foam base, but there are several tried-and-tested techniques for attaching materials to dry foam or twig bases. Objects such as ribbon and shells are best glued to the base using a hot glue gun or strong adhesive, while groups of decorative items, such as dried fruits and cherubs, should be wired to the wreath or pinned securely in place.

Flowers, leaves, fruit, and other decorative objects are often wired on a "double-leg mount," whereby a single wire is threaded through the item, bent into a hairpin shape, and the "legs" of wire twisted together.

## SUPPORTS

Wire is essential in wreath-making for holding the structure together, for anchoring a bed of moss to the wreath base, and for attaching decorative plant materials, fruits, objects, and ribbon bows. The two main types of wire used are floral wire and spool wire. Floral wire comes in a bewildering number of thicknesses and lengths, and its primary function is to reinforce the plant stem. As a general guideline, use fine-gauge floral wires to support delicate flowers and leaves and to wire up individual flowerets in bridal work. Medium-gauge floral wire is used to support medium-sized flowers and decorative objects, while heavy-gauge wires are reserved for large or heavy flowerheads or to create a hook to hang the finished wreath. Spool wire is useful for all kinds of binding work. It is used to bind flexible twigs and vines into wreath frames, to attach moss and heavy decorative items such as rope and driftwood onto purchased frames, and to bind individual stems and bunches of flowers and foliage onto a length of rope to make a garland. In addition to using these wires, you can also use U-shaped pins to fasten materials to a wreath base. These work particularly well if you want an item to sit flush with the frame, for example clumps of carpet moss or branches of pine, or when you are attaching a waterproof backing to a wreath. Either buy U-pins from

specialized suppliers, which can be prohibitively expensive, or make your own by cutting heavy-gauge floral wires into short lengths and bending them into shape with pliers.

In addition to attaching plant materials with wires, you can also use pearl-headed sewing pins to fasten garlands of flowers and trails of ivy and fresh fruits to tablecloths for special celebrations.

## USING ROPE, RIBBON, OR RAFFIA

The great choice of colorful ropes, ribbons, and raffias available to the wreath-maker is inspiring, and these materials will add the finishing creative touch to any display. Use your imagination to explore their use on wreaths, and experiment by attaching pleated folds of pretty ribbon to a wreath base with a hot glue gun or pinning a length of luxurious velvet or silk ribbon to a wreath frame to make a decorative hanging for the display. Alternatively, attach the ribbon after all the other materials have been added, wrapping trails of ribbon around the flowers and foliage, and finishing off with a bow. Colorful paper raffia can also be used to bind together hand-tied swags of flower stems that are then attached to a chair back with a generous length of ribbon and finished with a double bow, as in the Chair-back Decoration (see page 92).

## MAINTAINING THE FINISHED WREATH

Once you have created your wreath, garland, or swag of fresh flowers and foliage, keep it looking its best by spray-misting the plant materials and moss base with clean water on a daily basis. If the materials have been conditioned well beforehand, they should last for several days to a week within the display. For arrangements built on a foundation of fresh floral foam, keep checking that the foam is moist to the touch and add water only when it starts to dry out. For more long-lasting displays, choose plants that thrive on little water, such as succulents. These fresh displays will last for up to six weeks and are known as "living wreaths." To keep wreaths of dried flowers and foliage in good condition, keep them out of moist environments that may cause the plant materials to deteriorate. Try also to keep them away from direct heat and sunlight, which makes plant materials fade, and dust them at regular intervals to prevent dust particles from collecting on leaves and petals.

A decorative bow is easy to make: simply fold a ribbon into three loops and pinch the loops together in the middle. Take a second length of ribbon and tie it in a single knot around the center of the loops.

# plant directory

**Abies nobilis** (blue fir) p. 50
Evergreen trees with thick bluish needles, available between November and December for use in Christmas garlands and wreaths but can be bought throughout the year. The fir needles last well in displays. Before use, store branches in the cold, out of water.
**CARE** To condition, cut the ends of the stems with shears and remove the lower needles. To avoid shedding needles, buy food formulated for Christmas trees.

**Achillea** 'Moonshine' (yarrow) pp. 42, 78
Tall, summer-flowering perennial with attractive clusters of sulfur-yellow flowers and an aromatic fragrance. The dense flowerheads are useful for filling in arrangements. Cut or purchase the flowers when the flowerheads are at least three-quarters open.
**CARE** Remove all lower foliage, cut ½ inch (1 cm) from the stem base, and soak in a solution of flower food.

**Alchemilla mollis** (lady's mantle) p. 88
Perennial plant with lime-green flowers and pretty, fan-shaped leaves that grows to 16–20 inches (40–50 cm) high. Lady's mantle flowers between early and late summer. The flowers should be cut from the yard or purchased when most of the blossoms are already open.
**CARE** Cut the stem ends cleanly at an angle and then soak in water before using in displays.

**Anemone coronaria** (anemone) p. 38
Jewel-colored flowers in shades of blue, purple, red, and pink, with crowns of leaves around the petals on a leafless stem. Depending on the variety, they grow to 10–18 inches (25–45 cm) tall. Available from winter to early summer, they peak in spring.
**CARE** These thirsty flowers require no special treatment. Cut stem ends at an angle and soak in water before use.

**Anethum graveolens** (dill) p. 42
A strongly aromatic herb with feathery flowers that are excellent fillers in arrangements. Cut or purchase when the main umbel is fully grown.
**CARE** To condition, cut the stem ends at an angle, remove lower foliage, and place in clean water with flower food.

**Anthurium** (anthurium) p. 78
A tropical plant originating from the rain forests of Colombia, it is prized for its waxy green leaves and brightly colored or pale heart-shaped flowers. The flowers must be mature on purchase, and last up to three weeks.
**CARE** Cut the stem ends and soak in fresh water and flower food. Store out of cold temperatures, which tend to discolor the flowers.

**Capsicum** (chili pepper) p. 42
Chili seeds germinate in spring; by summer the plants produce shiny red or green fruits. Sold for most of the year as vegetables, dried chili peppers on stems are available in the fall and winter. They are useful for adding color and texture to festive wreaths and garlands.
**CARE** No special care instructions.

**Celosia argentea** (cockscomb) p. 92
Originally from tropical Africa, this flowering plant comes in two forms, which have either crests or plumes of brilliant deep red, magenta pink, or gold flowers.
**CARE** Trim the stem ends at an angle and condition with flower food. Remove all foliage.

**Centaurea cyanus** (bachelor's buttons) p. 84
There are many flowers in this family, but the bright blue annuals with small ruffled petals, available from spring to fall, are best known.
**CARE** Remove the foliage, cut the stem ends at an angle, and place in clean water with flower food.

**Clematis vitalba** (clematis vine) p. 60
Available in fall and winter when the clematis leaves have died back, leaving a vine stem. This vine is ideal for making wreath bases and for wrapping around wreaths and garlands. Collect from hedges or purchase from specialized florists.
**CARE** No special care instructions.

**Convallaria majalis** (lily-of-the-valley) p. 84
These sweet-scented, bell-shaped white flowers are available in late spring but can be bought throughout the year at a premium.
**CARE** Trim the stem ends and place them in water. Do not allow the stems to dry out.

**Cymbidium** (cymbidium orchid) p. 78
These popular orchids come on long or short stems and have waxy flowers in white, yellow, green, or pink.
**CARE** Cut ½ inch (1 cm) off the stem and place in tepid water with flower food. Do not place the flowers in direct sunlight or drafts.

**Delphinium** 'Blue Bees' (delphinium) p. 38
A perennial with tall stems carrying spikes of bell-shaped blue flowers. This variety is often treated before harvesting to make sure it will keep its flowers for up to ten days.
**CARE** Cut the stems and condition in clean water with flower food.

**Echeveria** (succulent) p. 20
These rosette-shaped succulents originate from Mexico, and there are more than 150 species sold as house and garden plants. They require little water and can survive for weeks in "living wreaths."
**CARE** Keep the root system intact when lifting from plant pots.

**Eustoma grandiflorum** (lisianthus) pp. 84, 88, 92, 96
These white or blue bell-shaped flowers are arranged on long stems as individual blooms or in panicles.
**CARE** Cut stem ends and condition in fresh water.

**Fagus** (beech) pp. 46, 88
An attractive green and copper foliage that is most spectacular in fall when the leaves turn beautifully rust colored.

**CARE** Preserve in glycerin for use in displays throughout the year.

*Fritillaria pinardii* (fritillary) p. 84
Delicate, bell-shaped flowers on slender stems, available in spring. This is one of the alpine varieties from Turkey, whose petals are gold on the inside and brown outside. Despite its fragile appearance, it survives well as a cut flower.
**CARE** Cut the ends of the stems at an angle and condition with water and flower food.

*Galax* (galax) p. 16
These glossy green heart-shaped leaves are available throughout the year, but turn dark red and mottled in autumn. Most galax leaves are harvested in the Appalachian Mountains and are distributed worldwide.
**CARE** Buy branches of leaves ready-preserved in glycerin.

*Gardenia* (gardenia) p. 60
Plants with glossy dark green leaves and highly scented waxy white flowers with either single or double blooms.
**CARE** Gardenias are most commonly sold as house plants and should be kept moist at all times with tepid water. Spray-mist the leaves and condition cut flowers in clean water and flower food before use.

*Hedera* (ivy)
pp. 38, 42, 64, 70, 74, 84, 88
This plant has many uses for the flower arranger. Young ivy plants produce trails of lobe-shaped leaves, while mature ivies produce flowers and attractive fruit.
**CARE** Bunches of fruiting ivy need their stems to be cut and placed in water for a few hours, while young ivy plants in pots should be conditioned overnight with water and flower food.

*Helianthus* (sunflower) p. 42
Originally from the southern and western regions of North America, this annual flower, with its golden-yellow petals and large dark center, has become very fashionable. There are single and double varieties, and it is available in a number of colors as well as the commonly known yellow.
**CARE** Cut stems at an angle and condition this thirsty flower overnight in fresh water.

*Hyacinthus* (hyacinth) p. 84
An extremely fragrant plant with spikes of bell-shaped flowers in a number of strong and pastel colors. It is popular as a potted bulb plant and now also as a cut flower. The cut flowers last up to 16 days, and each flower stalk can be divided up into individual flowerets and wired for use in headdresses and bridal bouquets.
**CARE** Cut stem ends at an angle and wipe away any excess sap.

*Hydrangea* (hydrangea)
pp. 56, 64, 88
Another useful flower for arrangers is the long-lasting, large-headed hydrangea. It is available in shades of pink, blue, or white.
**CARE** As cut flowers, hydrangeas will last for up to ten days but need constant spray-misting with water. If the flowers start to dry out, submerge the whole flowerheads in water to revive them. They can also be hung up to dry out.

*Lavandula* (lavender) p. 16
This densely growing plant produces fragrant mauve flowers and also has beautiful silver-gray stems and leaves. It can be hung up in bunches to dry and then stored and used for projects throughout the year.
**CARE** When using fresh, remove the lower foliage and place the stems in deep water. Change the water frequently and use flower food.

*Leucospermum cordifolium* (pincushion protea) p. 42
A South African flower commonly known as the pincushion because of its clustered red flowerhead. It lasts well out of water, which makes it a useful flower to use for hanging garlands.
**CARE** The woody stems should be cut at an angle and placed in fresh water and flower food.

*Lilium* (lily) p. 64
Large-headed scented lilies such as 'Casablanca' and 'Pompeii' are ideal for wreaths and garlands, as the flowers are long-lasting. To prevent permanent staining when people brush past the display, take care to remove the pollen-laden stamens in the center of the flowerheads.
**CARE** Cut the stem ends and place in water overnight.

*Lonicera* (honeysuckle vine)
pp. 24, 46, 64
Honeysuckle does not last well as a cut flower, but once the leaves have died back in autumn, the flexible vines can be harvested and used to make wreath bases.
**CARE** No special care instructions.

*Ornithogalum montanum* (starflower) p. 38
This spring-flowering bulb plant has a leafless stem and long-lasting, greenish-white star-shaped flowers.
**CARE** Cut stem ends and condition for a few hours in clean water before use.

*Pittosporum* (pittosporum) p. 88
Long-lasting evergreen foliage with small ovate leaves; some varieties have variegated leaves.
**CARE** Cut stem ends cleanly at an angle, then condition in fresh water.

*Polianthes tuberosa* (tuberose) p. 96
Stems of sweetly scented star-shaped cream flowerets that are popular the world over for bridal arrangements.
**CARE** Cut stem ends cleanly at an angle, and condition in water for a few hours before arranging.

*Ranunculus* (ranunculus) pp. 38, 84
These long-lasting colorful perennials resemble peonies and have either single or double blooms. They are available in winter to late spring.
**CARE** Cut stems and condition with flower food.

*Rosa* (rose) pp. 16, 56, 88, 92, 96
There is such a wide variety of roses and new shades are always being produced, presenting the flower arranger with a whole host of color combinations and types.
**CARE** Cut the stem ends at an angle and condition in water and flower food.

*Scabiosa* (scabious) p. 88
Perennial flower available in white and blue. Cut or buy scabious when the flowers are half open.
**CARE** Place stems in deep water and flower food for a few hours before use.

*Scilla* (bluebells) p. 38
A spring flower found growing in woodlands, but it should not be picked from the wild. Both

blue and white cultivated hybrids can be bought from florists in spring and will last up to a week in displays.
**CARE** Cut the stem ends at an angle and soak in fresh water and flower food for a few hours before arranging.

*Senecio cineraria* (dusty miller) p. 96
This attractive silver-gray foliage plant produces clusters of small yellow flowers.
**CARE** Cut stem ends at an angle and place in lukewarm water for a few hours before arranging.

*Stephanandra tanakae* (stephanandra) p. 78
These arching branches of foliage are available in autumn. The flexible branches are long-lasting and can be twisted around wreath bases to decorative effect.
**CARE** Cut the stems at an angle and soak in clean water.

*Symphoricarpos* (snowberry) p. 96
Used mainly for their pink and white pearly berries, these are among the first autumn berry plants to appear.
**CARE** Remove excess leaves and cut the stem ends at an angle before soaking in clean water.

*Tropaeolum* (nasturtium) p. 74
These long-lasting edible flowers have vivid orange or red petals that are used to decorate salads and to make table garlands.
**CARE** Cut the stem ends at an angle and place them in clean water. Make sure the flowers are free of aphids before use.

*Viburnum opulus* (guelder rose)
pp. 38, 56, 88
Lobed deep-green leaves, with fragrant white flowers and clusters of red berries.
**CARE** Cut stem ends at an angle and place in clean water with flower food.

*Viburnum tinus* (viburnum) p. 92
A very useful plant in winter, when other foliage and flowers are scarce. It produces pink buds and then forms pretty, white, star-shaped flowers between late fall and early spring. The foliage is available throughout the year for use in displays.
**CARE** Cut stem ends at an angle and place in clean water with flower food.

# resources

**WREATHS & FLORAL SUPPLIES**

In addition to the mail-order and specialty sources listed below, see the listing of craft-store chains and check local craft and floral supply shops for wreath forms and floral foam, tools, accessories, and supplies. Purchase live flowers from local flower markets, greengrocers, and supermarkets.

**FloraCraft**
One Longfellow Place
P.O. Box 400
Ludington, MI 49431
231-845-5127
Fax: 231-845-0240
www.floracraft.com
Distributors of wreath, topiary, and geometric forms made of Styrofoam™, extruded foam, and straw; also available are a vast array of floral supplies and accessories.

**High Country Floral**
P.O. Box 155
Carlton, WA 98814
509-923-2646
Fax: 509-923-2037
www.highcountryfloral.com
Here you can find preserved and stem-dyed wreaths, garlands, and arches; also preserved and stem-dyed baby's-breath in 18 colors, as well as a wide selection of other preserved and dried flowers and leaves, herbs, and spices.

**J & T Imports Dried Flowers**
P.O. Box 642
Solana Beach, CA 92075
858-481-9781
Fax: 858-481-0776
www.driedflowers.com
All sorts of dried and preserved flowers and foliage, including rosebuds by the pound. While they sell mainly to retail shops, they will fill credit card orders to the value of $50 or more.

**Loose Ends**
P.O. Box 20310
Keizer, OR 97307
503-390-7457
www.looseends.com
A wide selection of natural-fiber papers, ribbons, and botanicals, like seagrass, raffia, dried fruits, and fungi.

**Maple Ridge Supply**
9528 South Bolton Road
Posen, MI 49776
517-356-4807
Fax: 517-354-6664
www.mapleridgesupply.com
All sizes and shapes of metal wreath forms. They also make a simple tool called the Quik-Crafter™ to close the prongs on the forms easily and evenly.

**May Silk**
16202 Distribution Way
Cerritos, CA 90703
562-926-1818
A complete line of silk flowers, plants, foliage, trees, arrangements, and floral accessories is available here.

**Nature's Holler**
15739 Old Lowery Road North
Omaha, AR 72662
870-426-5489
Suppliers of grapevine wreaths, acorns, pods, pine cones, dried assorted weeds and grasses, color-blushed wheat, baby's-breath, moss, sunflowers, bamboo, and wood works: everything for dried arrangements.

**Tom Thumb Workshops**
59 Market Street
Onocock VA 23417
800-526-6502
Craft products, dried and pressed flowers, and skeletonized leaves, can be found here, and potpourri, herbs, spices, and essential oils.

**CRAFT-STORE CHAINS**

Most, if not all, of the supplies called for in this book can be found at any comprehensive craft store. These are the largest chains with stores around the country. Call the listed number or use your local Yellow Pages.

**Ben Franklin**
www.bfranklinstores.com
There is no centralized number for this franchised chain; look in your local Yellow Pages for the nearest outlet.

**Crafts and More**
A Division of Ames Department Stores
800-746-7263
www.ames.com

**Jo-Ann Stores, Inc**
216-656-2600; ask for Customer Service
www.joann.com
This chain operates under different names in different regions. Call to locate the affiliate nearest you.

**Frank's Nursery and Crafts**
313-564-2507; ask for Customer Service
www.franks.com

**Garden Ridge**
281-579-7901; ask for Customer Service
www.gardenridge.com

**Hobby Lobby**
405-745-1100; ask for Customer Service
www.hobbylobby.com

**MJ Designs, Inc.**
972-304-2200; ask for Customer Service
www.mjdesigns.com

**Michaels Stores, Inc.**
800-642-4235
www.michaels.com
Specialty retailer of craft items.

**A. C. Moore**
609-228-6700
www.acmoore.com
Craft superstores. Over 70 stores throughout Eastern US.

**Rag Shops, Inc.**
973-423-1303; ask for Customer Service
www.ragshop.com

**Treasure Island**
201-529-1771; press 2 for store locations
www.treasureislandstores.com

**Wal-Mart**
501-273-4000
www.walmart.com

**RIBBONS, TIES, & TRIMMINGS**

Ribbons and decorative cording and other tie trims are widely available in craft, variety, fabric, and sewing notions stores. The sources listed below provide a selection of the more unusual.

**Conso Products**
P.O. Box 326
Union, SC 29379
800-842-6676
www.conso.com
One of the largest distributors of decorative trims, cordings, ropings, tassels, and fringes in various fibers.

**Hancock Fabrics**
Call 877-Fabrics for a store near you.
www.hancockfabrics.com
Everything you need for projects involving sewing or fabrics, including adhesives.